In My Backyard

I SEE A SNAKE

By E. T. Weingarten

Gareth Stevens
PUBLISHING

Please visit our website, www.garethstevens.com. For a free color catalog of all our high-quality books, call toll free 1-800-542-2595 or fax 1-877-542-2596.

Library of Congress Cataloging-in-Publication Data

Names: Weingarten, E. T., author.
Title: I see a snake / E. T. Weingarten.
Description: New York : Gareth Stevens Publishing, [2019] | Series: In my backyard | Includes index.
Identifiers: LCCN 2018013378| ISBN 9781538228746 (library bound) | ISBN 9781538231807 (paperback) | ISBN 9781538231814 (6 pack)
Subjects: LCSH: Snakes–Juvenile literature.
Classification: LCC QL666.O6 W45 2019 | DDC 597.96–dc23
LC record available at https://lccn.loc.gov/2018013378

First Edition

Published in 2019 by
Gareth Stevens Publishing
111 East 14th Street, Suite 349
New York, NY 10003

Editor: Therese Shea
Designer: Sarah Liddell

Photo credits: Cover, pp. 1, 7, 24 (scales) Steve Bower/Shutterstock.com; p. 5 Kristian Bell/Shutterstock.com; p. 9 Matt Jeppson/Shutterstock.com; pp. 11, 24 (tongue) Plaskographer/Shutterstock.com; p. 13 Choke29/Shutterstock.com; p. 15 surin2514/Shutterstock.com; p. 17 Pazargic Liviu/Shutterstock.com; p. 19 Rich Carey/Shutterstock.com; p. 21 (left snake) Joe Farah/Shutterstock.com; p. 21 (right snake) KAMONRAT/Shutterstock.com; p. 23 Coy St. Clair/Shutterstock.com.

Printed in the United States of America

CPSIA compliance information: Batch #CW19GS: For further information contact Gareth Stevens, New York, New York at 1-800-542-2595.

Contents

I see a snake!

It has green scales.
It hides in the grass!

Snakes don't have ears.
They can see well.

Snakes smell with their tongue!

Snakes eat mice,
rats, birds, fish, frogs,
bugs, and eggs.
They eat other snakes!

Most snakes lay eggs.

Most snakes live
on the ground.
Some live in trees!

Sea snakes live in water!

There are over
3,000 kinds of snakes!

I watch the snake
in my yard!

Words to Know

scales

tongue

Index